LEVEL ONE
Sounding it out

All true and
unbelievable!

Learning to read. Reading to learn!

LEVEL ONE Sounding It Out Preschool–Kindergarten
For kids who know their alphabet and are starting to sound out words.

learning sight words • beginning reading • sounding out words

LEVEL TWO Reading with Help Preschool–Grade 1
For kids who know sight words and are learning to sound out new words.

expanding vocabulary • building confidence • sounding out bigger words

LEVEL THREE Independent Reading Grades 1–3
For kids who are beginning to read on their own.

introducing paragraphs • challenging vocabulary • reading for comprehension

LEVEL FOUR Chapters Grades 2–4
For confident readers who enjoy a mixture of images and story.

reading for learning • more complex content • feeding curiosity

Ripley Readers Designed to help kids build their reading skills and confidence at any level, this program offers a variety of fun, entertaining, and unbelievable topics to interest even the most reluctant readers. With stories and information that will spark their curiosity, each book will motivate them to start and keep reading.

Vice President, Licensing & Publishing   Amanda Joiner
Editorial Manager   Carrie Bolin

Editor   Jordie R. Orlando
Writer   Korynn Wible-Freels
Designer   Scott Swanson
Reprographics   Bob Prohaska
Production Design   Luis Fuentes

Published by Ripley Publishing 2020

10 9 8 7 6 5 4 3 2 1

Copyright © 2020 Ripley Publishing

ISBN: 978-1-60991-408-0

For more information regarding permission, contact:
VP Licensing & Publishing
Ripley Entertainment Inc.
7576 Kingspointe Parkway, Suite 188
Orlando, Florida 32819

Email: publishing@ripleys.com
www.ripleys.com/books
Manufactured in China in May 2020.

First Printing

Library of Congress Control Number:
2020937138

PUBLISHER'S NOTE
While every effort has been made to verify the accuracy of the entries in this book, the Publisher cannot be held responsible for any errors contained in the work. They would be glad to receive any information from readers.

PHOTO CREDITS

Cover © Jay Ondreicka/Shutterstock **3** © Jay Ondreicka/Shutterstock **4** © Fred Turck/Shutterstock **5** © MyTravelCurator/Shutterstock **6-7** © Jay Ondreicka/Shutterstock **8-9** Nick Garbutt/naturepl.com **10-11** Emanuele Biggi/naturepl.com **12-13** © vagabond54/Shutterstock **14-15** Sylvain Cordier/naturepl.com **16** Emanuele Biggi/naturepl.com **17** Nick Garbutt/naturepl.com **18-19** © Alex Edmonds/Shutterstock **20** © Will E. Davis/Shutterstock **21** © Dan_Koleska/Shutterstock **22-23** Daniel Heuclin/naturepl.com **24** © nickeverett1981/Shutterstock **25** © Marben/Shutterstock **26-27** imageBROKER/Alamy Stock Photo **28** (bl) © Luke Suen/Shutterstock **28-29** (t) imageBROKER/Alamy Stock Photo **28-29** (b) © Ethan Daniels/Shutterstock **29** (tr) © Pere Grau/Shutterstock **29** (br) © finchfocus/Shutterstock **30-31** © Rusty Dodson/Shutterstock **Master Graphics** Created by Scott Swanson

Key: t = top, b = bottom, l = left, r = right

All other photos are from Ripley Entertainment Inc. Every attempt has been made to acknowledge correctly and contact copyright holders and we apologize in advance for any unintentional errors or omissions, which will be corrected in future editions.

Ripley Readers

Animal Imposters!

All true and unbelievable!

RIPLEY

PUBLISHING

a Jim Pattison Company

Do you like to play pretend? Animals do!

They use disguises to hide from predators and to hunt for food!

Look out for that snake!
Wait, it's just a caterpillar!
No bugs or birds will
mess with him.

Did that leaf just move? It's not a leaf after all, it's a bug! It blends right in with the tree!

Wow, talk about camouflage! This gecko's brown tail looks just like a leaf!

It would be hard for a hungry bird to find it.

Be careful where you walk, killdeer lay their eggs on the ground!

Their white and black shells look like speckled rocks.

Can you find the eggs in this picture?

That is not a tree branch you are looking at. It is a bird!

Its feathers look like tree bark, don't you think?

Here is a disguise that will make you laugh: this frog looks like bird poop!

So does that spider! What funny camouflage!

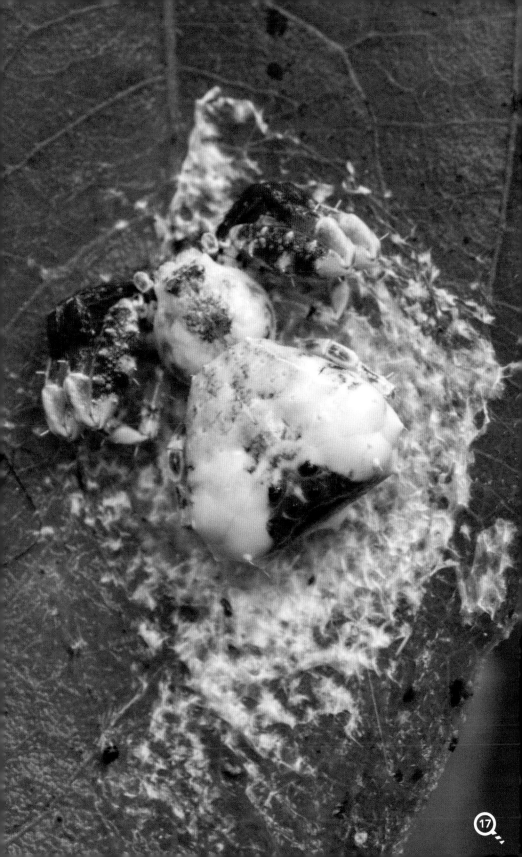

Better look out, little lizards,
or you will be food!

The vine snake has bright green
skin that blends in with the trees.
How many snakes can you find?

The kingsnake tricks its predators by looking like the venomous coral snake.

Kingsnake

Coral snake

Birds of prey don't want
a deadly dinner!

You can find animal disguises underwater, too!

This alligator snapping turtle has built-in bait: a red piece of skin that looks like a worm!

Red and white coral? Guess again!
It's a seahorse!

Green and brown seaweed?
Nope! It's a sea dragon!

An octopus can change
its color and its texture!

Sometimes it's bumpy,
sometimes it's smooth.

Can you find one
lying on the reef?

A lionfish is venomous, but don't be fooled. This is a mimic octopus!

See how it can make itself look like a starfish and a flounder, too?

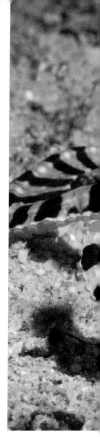

Pretending to be a starfish!

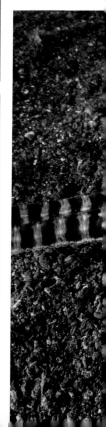

Lionfish

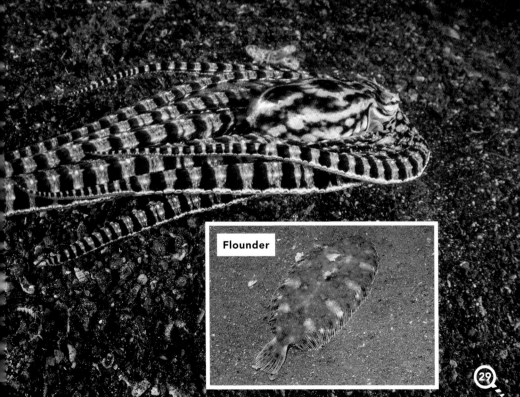

Flounder

There are all kinds of amazing disguises in nature!

Can you make up an animal imposter of your own?

Ripley Readers

Ready for More?

Ripley Readers feature unbelievable but true facts and stories!

LEVEL ONE
Sounding it out

LEVEL TWO
Reading with help

LEVEL THREE
Independent reading

LEVEL FOUR
Chapters

For more information about
Ripley's Believe It or Not!, go to www.ripleys.com